# This is Her

## A Journey from Brokenness to Wholeness

### Rashonda Key

Copyright © 2021 Rashonda Key

ISBN: 978-0-578-89333-4

Published by Rashonda Key

This book may not be copied or reprinted for commercial gain or profit. No part of this publication may be reproduced, distributed, or transmitted in any form or by any means, or stored in a database or retrieval system without prior written permission of the compiling author.

Scripture quotations marked "ASV" are taken from the American Standard Version Bible (Public Domain).

Scriptures marked NKJV are taken from the New King James Version®. Copyright © 1982 by Thomas Nelson. Used by permission. All rights reserved.

Edited by Ready Writer Services, LLC

# **Dedication**

I want to dedicate this book to young men & women struggling with painful experiences, not knowing how to break that cycle of Brokenness. This book is to empower you to strive for Wholeness by allowing the love of God to completely restore you and give you the peace that He desires you to have so that you can fully walk in your purpose and be great.

# Acknowledgements

*First, I have to thank my Lord and Savior, Jesus Christ, for giving me the boldness and courage to write this book. I'm so grateful that He saw something in me, that I couldn't see in myself.*

*To my amazing husband, Vince, for your love and support and space to take this journey. You are my greatest supporter, always so encouraging. Can't imagine doing life with anyone else. I always say that your love changed my life. Thank you for loving me.*

*To my wonderful gifts, my children, Kayla, Kamryn & Kaden. Thank you for being understanding and giving me the space to take this journey. Mommy loves you with everything. You 3 are my greatest accomplishments. So grateful God chose me to be your mommy.*

*To my parents, Vernon & Rosemary, for your patience, understanding, and love as I take this journey. Mom, thank you for the amazing foundation that you set for me which has shaped me into the woman of God I am today. Dad, thank you for being my Rock, no matter what life brings. I'm confident you got me, and I'll come through stronger than ever because you're always there to love and guide me through.*

*I am forever grateful to my Bishop & Pastor, John & Isha Edmondson. So thankful for my set place. Thank you for the consistent love for your spiritual sons & daughters and for always empowering us to walk in our purpose and our calling. Love you both so much.*

*To my Squad, my beautiful sisters, I'm a better woman because of each of you.*

*So thankful for all the amazing women/mentors whom God placed in my life to help hold me accountable and ensure that this book happen.*

# *Fruit of the Spirit*

*"But the fruit of the Spirit is love, joy, peace, longsuffering, kindness, goodness, faithfulness, meekness, self-control; against such there is no law."*

Galatians 5:22-23 ASV

An outward display of the Holy Spirit's work within Christians. Love, Joy, Peace, Patience, Kindness, Goodness, Faithfulness, Gentleness, and Self-control. This fruit of the Spirit demonstrates the character of a life submitted to God. It has always been important for me to live by this scripture in the Bible. In everything I do, I always try to display this fruit. It's important for me to tell my story because it wasn't always easy to have the fruit of the Spirit within my heart. There were many opportunities, in fact, to display the complete opposite. However, I want people to know that you will experience seasons in your life in which the enemy's plan is for you to be left broken and feeling like you're unable to walk with God or be used by Him. That might be the enemy's plan, but I am living proof that his plan doesn't prosper.

My story in *This is Her* is designed to show you what brokenness looks like but more importantly what the journey to becoming whole looks like as well. And how the Love of God is greater than any broken moment or painful experience you've had to face. I've decided to share my story with you now, in this season, because God said that my story needed to be told, that there were those who needed to read it. He helped me understand that everything I've experienced, everything that brought me pain, was just a part of my testimony and was placed in my life to help me grow and make me a better person. It was for purpose.

In the moment, no one wants to go through anything that's going to cause pain. Pain and heartache are not enjoyable. But when you invite God into your life, He's able to show you why some of those things were necessary and how it will shape you into the person that He destined you to be. We all have a purpose and, sometimes, those broken moments show us exactly who we are and what we're called to do. My hope is that my story breeds hope in others who may have been rejected and left feeling broken. I hope that, after reading this, they tap into the greatness that is inside of them, and they use that pain to propel them as they walk in their own journey from brokenness to wholeness…and be great.

# *This is Her*

Who is Rashonda? If you asked me this question today, I would say I'm a God-fearing woman who works very hard to keep the fruit of the Spirit in my heart daily. God is the center of my life and has blessed me with an amazing heart for people. It truly brings me so much joy to see people happy. People often say to me, "You are always smiling." I know deep down they question how I can always be that happy. Truth is, I've dealt with and still deal with a lot of drama in my life, but I have never been a person that allows the drama to get the best of me. There are times I may be dealing with things internally, but I made a choice to always let God's love for me shine on the outside.

I love to celebrate others and see people do well. Building up and encouraging others is something that comes very natural to me. I've been this way since I was a child, but never understood why. In my early teen years, there was a pastor who spoke over my life at a church service. My grandmother and my mother were both there. I remember the pastor coming down from the pulpit and asked me to stand. He said there was a call on my life to the point of admonishing me not to get caught up in what was happening around me. It would be crucial for me to focus on that call, but the enemy wanted to pervert Gods plan by allowing painful and traumatic things to take place in my life. Yet God still got all the glory out of every situation I faced. Instead of crushing my spirit, everything that I have ever gone through caused me to love harder and helped shape me into the woman that I am today.

Growing up, in school I was liked by everyone for the most part, and I never really had any major issues with people. It was my nature to befriend everyone, whether you were popular or a loner. I always tried to see the good in everyone. The amazing heart God gave me allowed me to totally change the dynamic of high school for one of my friends. In the beginning, the young boy had no friends. I remember that no one liked him or wanted him around, they wanted nothing to do with him. I don't know why people treated him so badly, but I was never one to follow the crowd. I knew he was adopted and had a different life than many others. I don't know if that's what drew me to him, but with the heart that God gave me I felt led to help make a difference for him. We became friends and, as we got closer, I began to see how smart and amazing he was as a person. Getting to know him became a joy, and he became one of my best friends. God's love for him showed through me in such a major way, helping him to have an amazing high school experience. People started seeing him differently, they started liking him as a person. All it took was one heart being open and willing to give someone a chance and help them out. Kids can be so mean and I'm grateful I was strong enough to have a heart for God and a mind of my own. Because of this, he was so thankful; and, in return, he helped me accomplish many great things as well. He was extremely smart, and he was able to help me study for my SAT to get into college. So, God knew exactly what we both needed. I was able to help this person have a great high school experience without the pressure and he helped me accomplish my goal for my SAT; and, together, we built a great friendship.

You see, I've always wanted to see the best in people and see them shine in whatever way I could. So, who is Rashonda? Well, everything that I am is because of God. My heart totally belongs to Him, whatever He says I will do. Because of the heart God has given me, I'm able to be an amazing mom to my children. I'm able to love and cover my husband with such joy. I'm able to be a loving and supportive daughter to my parents and a good friend to those with whom God allows me to connect.

## *Broken Beginnings*

Many of us have experienced broken moments which the enemy has designed to destroy us. The enemy will use anything to take you off the course that God has for you because he hates you, he hates us. He does this by allowing you to feel rejected and broken, especially, from those who are closest to you. Mother, father, siblings, grandparents, children, close friends, spouses, etc. So, what does it mean to be rejected? To me, being rejected is a feeling of nonacceptance by those you thought would accept you, or the refusal of one's feelings or emotions. When someone is in a place of rejection, it opens up an opportunity for the enemy to control your thoughts, emotions, and even actions. Many times, when I was experiencing rejection, it was difficult for me to know my own worth and the power God gave me within. If you're not careful, these moments can prevent you from ever moving forward in life and ultimately destroy you.

*"The thief does not come except to steal, and to kill, and to destroy. I have come that they may have life, and that they may have it more abundantly,"*

John 10:10 (NKJV)

In the Bible, the Apostle John tells us that the enemy comes to steal, kill, and destroy; that is his mission! But God's plan was to give us life more abundantly. God never intended for us to stay stagnant in a place of hurt, rejection, or brokenness even when the enemy tries to use that for his mission. God intends for us to heal from our hurts so that we move to where He has orchestrated our lives to go and not carry those hurts to others.

## A Mother's Attention

I have always admired my mother for her strength, independence, and love for God. She is the most hardworking person I've ever met. My mom would often work 12 hour shifts for days back to back, taking double shifts. Two of the greatest things I learned from her is how to be an independent woman and how to trust God. She raised us on her own with little to no help. She worked so hard to give us nothing but the best. She always made sure we had everything that we needed. She made sure that, when we stepped out for school or any outing, we were well put together. She would often say we represented her, and ensured we were on point.

My love for fashion truly comes from this woman, by herself and herself alone, she always desired for us to have nice things. I would often think that all the nice things she gave us were how she expressed her love, or that it was sometimes her way of saying sorry. In my adulthood, many times I thought, 'Yes it was really nice to have things but really I could have benefited more from simply having a conversation with her.' But instead of having a conversation when things weren't so good, we would get really nice clothes and material things.

Overtime, I grew to understand that this was her way of showing her love.

My childhood experiences were not always so favorable. In fact, most of it was infused with a spirit of rejection. For most of my childhood I felt abandoned, 3rd grade in particular was the worst for me. When I was in 3rd grade, my mom moved away to Florida with her new husband (her 2nd husband) and my little sister. She had left me behind to be raised by my grandmother. Imagine being 10 years old and having your mother leave you to start a new life without you. This experience left me feeling confused, broken, and sad. I never really understood why I couldn't go. If it was explained, I probably still wouldn't have understood why I couldn't be with my mom. To me, no answer would have taken away the pain and rejection that I felt at that time. I don't know if anyone stopped to think about the damage that was caused by leaving me behind. All I know is that I carried this hurt around for many years which, in turn, left a huge hole in my heart. I always felt like I was the kid that no one wanted.

At the time, I felt that my grandmother perceived I was a burden to care for, especially since she was already caring for at least 3 other younger cousins and other family members.

Leaving me created a void and a tremendous lack of trust. Trying to understand how a mom could leave her child behind was extremely difficult to do. I felt like my mom was away enjoying her new life with her new husband and their new baby, and I just didn't fit into that perfect family picture. This caused me to suffer in a major way in school; my grades were horrible. I got into fights and became such an angry kid because I was hurting inside and had no one with whom to share my feelings. I will say that I am eternally grateful for my godmother in this time of my childhood. She was the only one who actually checked in with me and asked if I needed to talk. I'm forever appreciative for her care then and, even now, as an adult.

Still, as a child, I longed for my mother. As a result, I acted out in school hoping that I would get my mother's attention and make her come back, but instead I had to repeat the 3$^{rd}$ grade. I still remember the night she left. She came to my bed to say goodbye and tell me that she loved me. She loved me? But she was leaving me? How could any of it make sense to a 10-year-old girl?

I don't think I said anything back to her. But I remember crying the entire night. That, for me, was one of the worst moments of my childhood. It was around September or October, on a cool fall night, around 11:00 pm. I was in bed and she came into my room to say goodbye. All I recalled from her words were, "Mommy is about to leave, I love you and will see you soon when you come to visit." After that the words started to muffle. The only thought in my head was that she was leaving without me. I couldn't even speak or utter any sounds. Tears fell from my face as she spoke. She kissed me goodbye, and I said nothing. Without a second thought, she left that room and seemingly out of my life. I didn't sleep at all that night. I pulled the blanket over my head to hide the anger and sadness I felt in my heart. I really thought that my display would make her stay. It was like no one even thought about how this would make me feel. They just did what was best for them. I didn't even have time to prepare for this transition. In the blink of an eye, my world, my reality shifted. When she was saying goodbye to me, she seemed sad and it didn't seem like it was easy for her to do. Which made me all the more confused. She obviously didn't want to leave me behind, so why did she? I often wondered.

Eventually, my mom came back. She stayed in Florida for a little over a year. But the seeds of abandonment had already been sown. She was in a very abusive marriage and, when they moved away, I guess he saw that as an opportunity to get her away from her family so he can be even more abusive. He abused her verbally, mentally, and physically. She initially left him, but he followed her back to New Jersey, and she took him back. Living in the house with him was excruciatingly hard. My sister and I were exposed to all the abuse and it caused me to really dislike him. There would be times that the fights would escalate, and he would really hurt my mom physically. I would have to call the police at least once a month to stop him from hurting her. I was around 11 years old when I was exposed to the abuse he would bring on my mom. I was traumatized because this was the first time I ever witnessed a man hitting a woman. No young and impressionable child should ever have to see this. At times, I really thought he would kill her and maybe even worse, do the same to me and my sister. I was even more fearful for me, after all I wasn't his biological child and I felt that maybe he resented me to a degree.

It bothered me that my mother took this abuse and did nothing to change it. I guess she lacked the strength to leave him or put her and her children first, back then. Many times, after I would call the police, she would forgive him almost immediately and let him back into the house, not thinking about the damage it was doing to us. I never really understood why she reacted this way, when he clearly was causing harm to her physically and emotionally. I would often wonder if she accepted this because of what she was exposed to growing up; or because she loved him or (which I discovered more as an adult than a kid) maybe being alone was a scary place for her. In my young mind, I felt as though being a wife took precedence over being a mother at times. Although this may not have been the case, this is truly how I felt. I mean, as a mother, who would want their kids exposed to certain things that could traumatize your children? We witnessed this almost every day. I remember crying many nights, unable to fathom why she would let someone like that stay in our lives. His addiction to drugs was really bad, which is what she believed caused him to act the way he would.

I grew from dislike to hatred in my heart towards him, and the feeling was mutual for him. Growing up with him in the house created a toxic environment for everyone. I don't recall ever seeing him in a loving way. He never had anything positive to say to us or my mom. He was always angry and mean, and he would call her all types of names. He tore her down daily with his words and actions. Because of all this, my attitude was the worst towards him. Even though I had issues with her, she was still my mom and it bothered me that someone would treat her so badly. I often asked myself, 'Why do I care so much? Clearly she liked to be treated this way.' I would regularly think that she must not have cared that much about us to have us in that toxic environment and I was right to have felt those things inside my heart because those were my true feelings. It was natural for me to hate my environment and have moments when I hated her for not choosing us. But, again, because of the heart that God has given me, I could never hate the person that gave me life, and who worked so hard everyday to provide for me. Maybe some would, but I just couldn't bring myself to hate her. I have always considered myself her protector. No one else protected her, so I felt it was my role. It caused me so much pain to watch someone treat her so badly.

No matter how mad I was at her, I was never going to let anyone hurt her. I always had a strong love for my mom and was patient, hoping that one day she would see that she deserved so much greater. Because of the way he would treat her, I would have such an attitude with this man. Many times, I would hear them in another room discussing me and my behavior. And because of my attitude, he would say, "Your daughter is so disrespectful," and after all the protection I would bring to her, I felt betrayed when she would yell at me for my attitude towards him! She would say that I had a bad attitude and I needed to show him more respect. Her words were so painful at times. She would say things like, "I can't wait for you to turn 18 so you can get out." Afterwards, she would ask if I wanted to go shopping and buy me something nice, imagine my confusion. The shopping sprees were always just a temporary fix with no substance for change or healing to take place.

My perception (whether right or wrong) was that she chose her husband before her children. Never stopping to consider why I gave him so much attitude. First, he took her away from me and moved to Florida. Then, he comes back addicted to drugs and abuses my mom in every way. Of course I'm going to have an attitude and be resentful. It was hurtful to watch her go through that pain and push me away, all for him, when I was the one that always tried to protect her.

I always felt that being a wife was what my mom most desired, more than anything. Ephesians 5:33 tells us in so many words that a husband must love his wife as himself, and good wife values her husband's opinion, admires his values and character, and is considerate of his needs such as the need for self-confidence and the need to be needed. But it didn't have to be one or the other, wife or mom. I believe one can be both a wife and a mother, and it's not necessary to choose one over the other. I think certain situations make a demand of what's important in that moment. For example, I can be wife, but not stand by silently if my husband does something that puts my children in danger or causes them harm. I think just because it's the husband's role to lead the house doesn't mean I follow him into sin. The Bible is clear on that! And I felt that in so many ways my mom couldn't separate the two.

Now on the other hand, she was strong when it came to preventing him from causing any physical harm to us. He has never laid a hand on any of us. I think that was the only time I would see her find strength - if he tried yelling at her children. That was something she would boldly stand up to and back him all the way down which also confused me. She wouldn't allow him to say anything to us but would allow him to disrespect her in every way. That's how it was no matter how badly he treated her, she would love and support him 100 percent. I just didn't get it and she never tried talking to me to help me understand what I was feeling.

One of the most painful moments for me was when I gave birth to my first child. Her husband called and wanted her to come home. I was almost 7 cm dilated, and she told me that she had to go. She left me and my husband alone as I had to experience childbirth on my own, without my mother, because her husband said it was late and he wanted her home. Even thinking back to when I was in middle school and high school. I ran track for 6 years and became a very accomplished athlete. By the time I graduated high school, I had broken my high school's record and became State Champion. However, in all that, I never had the support that others had. I never had any family come to see me perform. Which made me feel so sad in those moments. The only support that I had was from my coach and teammates. They would often be the ones cheering me on during each race.

My mom did come to one race in my senior year. I was so excited to see her in the bleachers. She was actually going to watch me race, but then I remember that, as I was about to run my first race of the night, my mom's husband apparently got into an argument with someone at the meet and said it was time to go. So, imagine me super excited that my mom was finally here to see me run and, just as my event starts, she said she had to go. I was so unbelievably devastated. This was my senior year and she had missed all my previous meets; and I only had 2 more meets to compete in, which she was also not able to attend due to work. Once again, she allowed him to ruin every possible good moment for us. Any opportunity to share in a joyful mother/daughter moment – diminished. The pain I felt being rejected by mom was shattering, not understanding why I never felt that mother's love. I know that she loved me and did her best, but back then, it just felt like all the love she had she gave to her husband. My mom was a woman of God and of great faith, but I often wondered, 'If she loved God so much why would she stay in a relationship that brought so much pain?' I wondered why she couldn't trust God to make her whole and recognize her self-worth. Why couldn't she see the pain that we were experiencing?

When I was younger, I would intentionally say things to get her attention, hoping that anything I said would cause her to want to sit down and talk to me. I would constantly say how much I hated him and how much I hated living in the house with them, and that I'd rather go live with my dad. I was silently screaming for her attention, saying and doing things that I thought would get her attention. Hoping and praying that she'd hear or see my desperate cry for my mother, but nothing worked. So, when I was a teenager, I became very curious and lost my virginity at the age of fourteen. I thought that, once she found out what I had done, she would really pay closer attention to what was going on with me. I was convinced that the way I was acting would draw some form of attention from her, even if it wasn't the good kind.

I often think back to where I was as a kid and compare myself to my now almost 14-year-old daughter. I thank God that I've been able to be a good mother to her because I cannot imagine her thinking the way I thought at that age and yearning for attention. My daughter's thoughts are so pure and innocent; and if she ever feels any type of way or has any concerning thoughts, I am right there for her. It makes a huge difference in our kids' lives when parents take the time to check in with them and ensure all is well. The difference is that I had so much built up inside, I never really had the chance to express how these things truly made me feel. I never had the opportunity to let them out open and honestly, then to receive guidance and compassion. Therefore, I saw myself carrying that into my adult life. There were instances where I would lash out and do things, again hoping that, at some point, she would see that her daughter was still carrying this pain. Praying she would say, "Wow. We really need to sit down and talk." But God had to deal with me because He would not want me to respond to my pain by lashing out at my mom or putting myself in situation that could further cause me harm. Losing my virginity so young caused me to grow up way sooner than I should have and experience heartache that could have been avoided if I had that outlet to talk about my feelings. I know God had better for me at that time and didn't want me lashing out and doing things to hurt her like she hurt me.

All of this showed me that I was still broken. In my adulthood, I had to ask myself, 'Why does the pain of my past still bother me? Why am I still broken?' I realized I was still harboring the pain and rejection from my childhood, even though I was married and had already given birth to our first child. For me, when I came to this realization, I understood that I couldn't effectively and wholeheartedly destroy generational curses until I was free from things that had me bound. This would begin the struggle of letting things go so I could be the emancipator our generation desperately needed. There was a time when she would try to embrace me in my adult life, and I felt myself pulling back. The love I hopelessly sought when I was a child, I now couldn't even receive as an adult. I wish, having the relationship she had with God, that she would have been more sensitive to the pain that was inflicted on her children. But then the Lord reminded me that no one is perfect, not even (and especially) our parents. We're only human and we are going to make mistakes.

I never knew anyone that loved God more and lived their life trying to please God more than my mom.

But we all fall short and we don't always get it right. That's what God reminded me of, and it gave me peace. I believe, if we would have had a chance to express how her actions and choices made us feel, true healing could have taken place sooner. However, because this never happened, I feel like we all put walls up to protect our hearts which only made things worse. I know, personally, I never wanted to put up those walls, but I didn't want to keep getting hurt either. I wanted to feel her love and embrace; and I wanted her to utterly understand the pain we were feeling and come to a place of true genuine love from her heart. I wanted to be at a place of having no expectations and just trying to love through the hurt and pain. I know that I must love and honor my mother despite everything that I may feel that she did wrong because God's word tells us to. But to do this, I really had to trust that God had a plan for us all. Once I took my hands off the situation and stopped trying to fix things myself, God was able to work on my mom. This was not an easy process, though. I also think it truly does matter where you go to church. Upon hearing the teaching of my Bishop and Pastor, I learned that I must remove expectations from people. I was constantly expecting my mother to "get it" and placing expectations that weren't hers to meet. I also learned that true forgiveness is not about the person, but more about me. I came to terms with the fact that even if we never had the opportunity to sit down and discuss our issues, I had to trust God's plan for my life.

At that point, I just accepted her for where she was in her life and understand that it may not be easy for her to sit and hear us talk about all the mistakes she made. Truthfully, it's not easy for any of us to hear about our mistakes, but God is gracious in how He shows us. And, for her, it seemed like revisiting some of those things from the past may have been hard for her. So, I was just grateful to God for His unconditional love for me. Because it's His love that kept me as a child and raised me up to always see the good in people and love them in spite of them. I will always love and honor my mother, earnestly. We're at a wonderful place now because I've learned to just love her and pray for her with no expectations. When I released the expectations, a huge weight was lifted off me. I was able to accept her for where she was and allow God to work on her and me. Through this, restoration was able to begin.

Presently, being able to reconcile with my mom has meant everything to me. Once I released the expectations, God was able to come in and restore the relationship. I also feel that once my mom was no longer broken herself, she had more love to give to us. I now understand that she has always loved us with her all; but because of what she was given, she didn't always know how to display the love that she had on the inside. I'm so grateful for the change and healing that God has brought her through. It's so astonishing to see her smile and be happy and whole.

I'm especially grateful for the heart-felt conversations that we've shared which have opened the door for us to recreate our own mother-daughter relationship. Being able to share my heart with her has been so freeing, and this has brought so much healing. The beauty in us recreating our relationship, is that now that we both have committed to allowing God's love to shine through. And because we made this decision God has been able to take control. We both refuse to allow the enemy to rob us of having a mother-daughter bond that is significant to us. We're not trying to have what others have, rather focused on cultivating what God desires us to have.

## *Prayer for Mother/Daughter Relationships*

Dear Lord,

I thank you for entrusting me with the gift of my beautiful daughter. May I live a virtuous life before her where she awards me the honor of calling me blessed. (Prov 31:28) Grant me the wisdom I need to train her in the way that she should go. May she grow to know more of You each day. I ask that You bless my relationship with my daughter. I ask that You forgive us for any negative thoughts, words, or actions we had against each other. I pray that we love each other unconditionally with the agape love that is written in Your Word. (1 Cor 13:4-7)

Father, please walk with my daughter wherever she may go. Watch, guide, comfort, and protect her. May she feel Your ever-loving presence around her and be at peace knowing that no weapon formed against her will ever prosper. Lord, only You know the marvelous purpose and plans that you have for my daughter. May she know, trust, and obey Your voice. Lead her along the right paths and help her to have an amazingly abundant life that exceeds anything she could ever imagine. In Jesus' mighty name, I pray. Amen.

## Daddy's Little Girl

I've always been a daddy's girl. My dad and I have had a special bond since day one and I have always loved my father. Initially, my parents both worked extremely hard to be the best parents they could. My father even quit high school to work and prepare for my arrival. You see, in their senior year of high school, my parents got pregnant with me. Although they were very young, they took parenting seriously at that time. Everyone knew I was my dad's little princess. Unfortunately, when I was 2, my parents decided to end their relationship and just try co-parenting. The separation was difficult for my dad which then brought on many challenges, thus changing the dynamic of our own relationship. I didn't see him as often anymore. Then, my mom got married to her 1st husband. Her 1st husband was a really nice guy from what I can remember. He loved me very much too, though I wasn't his child. My dad also eventually got married and everyone was living their lives. A few years later, my mom's husband died in a car accident, so I no longer had him in my life. Though he was not my biological father, I felt an emptiness because I no longer had a father figure in my life.

It was shortly after my stepdad died that my mom married her 2nd husband whom I never looked at as a father figure. I already mentioned earlier how I felt about this man's presence in our lives. Still the absence of my stepdad and not seeing my biological dad anymore made me feel empty. I would fantasize about the father-daughter bond I once had with my dad, praying to someday have that again in some form or fashion. Having a father figure was important to me because I longed for the provider and, most of all, protector. To all the fathers out there, you are the foundation on which the generations after you are built. While motherhood is amazing, I feel there are things only the father can bring to the relationship between a parent and a child. For me, I needed my father to consistently be there to show me the true example of fatherhood. If I was to ever have children, I needed to know how to normalize that father/daughter or father/son bond. Growing up, it hurt to see other fathers celebrating their children. In all the track meets I participated, I never had the feeling of winning a race and being able to run to my daddy's embrace and hear him say, "I'm proud of you baby girl." I missed those moments of going to homecoming dances and proms and having my father see me off or give me that "talk" about boys and what to look out for...I missed all of that.

Overall, I just missed the time we could have spent together on the weekends. Just the two of us. Although my dad was in my life, initially, it was not consistent. My dad was great at stopping in to drop off really nice gifts. He would promise that we would start spending more time together, but never fulfilled that promise. I recall moments when he would call and tell my mom he was picking me up for the weekend. She would have my stuff all packed up and I would be so excited to spend time with him. As I stood at the end of my driveway, I would wait hour after hour, watching the cars pass by and thinking the next car was his. As it got darker, my mom would call me back into the house and say, "I guess he's not coming." I felt completely heartbroken. This occurred over, and over again. Each time it happened, I would still get excited at the thought of being with him. Though, in the back of my mind, I couldn't help but think if I would be disappointed yet again.

Time. It was his time that I craved. My dad was still broken, though, from the split with my mom and he was busy with his new family now. His wife had 3 kids and he became their stepfather. I felt like his new family got all his time and energy because that is where most of his efforts went. Being his firstborn child, I was heartbroken to get this response from him. I had heard the stories about how much he was into me when I was first born. How deeply involved he was with my arrival. But I felt the same feeling of abandonment that I had experienced with my mom. It seemed that everyone was happy with their new families and I was the outcast, the fifth wheel. I felt as though I had been kicked out of the family club.

However, in this situation, I just had to overcome unforgiveness with my dad because there were so many broken promises over the years. Still, for some reason no matter how much I was hurt, he could do no wrong in my eyes. The love I had for my father just felt unconditional, he just needed to grow as a father. I grew up getting a lot of gifts and material things, but also broken promises. And this was the season in my life when I hated living in my house with my $2^{nd}$ stepdad and I wanted to be with my dad so badly. However, because of the emptiness and the void I felt, I became distant from him. When I was growing up, my dad made mistakes with me by not being there at different times when I really needed him. He missed so many important moments in my life, almost all of my many track meets (I think he might have come to one). He missed both high school and college graduations, and proms; all of which left me hurt and disillusioned. Truly grateful for my mom because she was there for my graduations and proms and made those moments memorable for me. All the gifts here and there didn't make up for the big moments when I needed my dad. But as he grew to be a better man, he actually became a better dad as well.

Even with all the mistakes my dad made, he has always remained so special to me. We always had a special bond that only got better as my dad grew and made changes in his life. I'm grateful for his ability to realize those necessary changes and his willingness to make them. He became more present in our lives. There was a time when I didn't know if my dad and I would ever have the relationship I desired for us. But with time and growth, God worked on us both and I began to see my dad the way God sees him. This helped me understand my dad in a greater way. He sought out to pursue a better relationship with me. And after having my two daughters, I started noticing the change. He was focused on being the best grandfather he could be and righting the wrongs he made with me. Over the years, we've had many discussions about our past and I was finally able to hear his perspective on where his mindset was. I gained so much appreciation for his transparency. It brought so much clarity and peace to those hurts I was carrying. To this day, I know I can talk to my dad about anything without judgement, and we have one of the strongest bonds ever.

I understand that God loves us in spite of the many mistakes we make. During this time of healing and restoration, even my dad's relationship with God grew. He really was committed to being a better man and father. Our love for one another and the amazing bond that we had was restored. We shut the enemy's plan down, the devil wanted me to be fatherless and my children to be without their grandfather. But I can honestly say that we overcame every battle that was thrown at us. What the devil meant for evil God turned it around for our good. And because I know this isn't easy, it's not magic, I want to share what we did as we worked toward restoration. I fought by keeping the lines of communication open and never closing myself off from the possibility of reconciliation in our relationship. My relationship with God led to me shutting down the enemy's plan as well. The more I let things go, the more I saw myself develop in God. The more I grew in God's desire for my life, the stronger my father-daughter bond became. This was not an easy process. There were times when he would break promises and not show up or be there for me. Each time that would happen, I would feel the progress we had made taking steps backward. But we fought back hard, we pressed, and now my dad and I have the greatest relationship a girl could ever ask for.

He is my rock; he has gotten me through some of the toughest moments in my adult life. I don't know what I would have done without him. And he is hands down the best grandfather ever. If it took him making mistakes as a dad to later take the time to learn and grow in how to become the best Pop Pop, then it was all worth it. My kids and I now have the fairy tale relationship I always wanted with my father. I now have the best dad and they have the greatest grand pop, and we wouldn't change him for anything. Some people may carry resentment in their hearts because of their situation with their father, but trust me, resentment only hurts you. The nature of my heart isn't built to hold resentment long term. Although I made the decision to forgive long ago, it took a while to earn the trust. But my dad worked overtime to rebuild that trust without me even asking. This is why we have the relationship that we have today. I can only thank God for that. And God can do it for you too. Whatever brokenness you've experienced from your father, make the decision to forgive and let go of any resentment or bitterness. Once you do, God is the Restorer, He will do the rest and the work will begin!

## *Prayer for Father/Daughter Relationships*

Dear God,

How great is Your love that You have lavished on us that we should be called Your children (1John 3:1). Thank You that You are our Abba Father. Thank You for being our perfect example of a father's love. For You loved us so much that You gave Your only begotten Son for us that we would not perish but have everlasting life (John 3:16).

Because of Your great love for us, You bankrupted heaven so that we may be reconciled back to You through Your gift of salvation. We are Your beloved, the apple of Your eye whom You love with an everlasting love! Thank You that nothing could ever separate us from Your love.

Lord, thank You, that even if we do not have a relationship with our earthly father or if they have transitioned to eternity, Your word says that You are a father to the fatherless (Psalm 68:5). We thank You that You will never leave or forsake us. We praise You because there is nothing that can ever separate us from Your love (Romans 8:38); You love us with an everlasting love, and You draw us in with unfailing kindness (Jeremiah 31:3). Thank You for the intimacy that comes with being Your child. You knew us before we were formed in our mother's womb and shaped us, protected us, purposed us, and loved us! You know what we stand in need of before we can even ask, and You say that no good thing will You withhold from us!

Father, thank You that there is nowhere we can go that You're not there. If we ascend to heaven You are with us and if we make our beds in hell You are there (Psalms 139:7-8). And when we find ourselves in a position like the prodigal son, you love us so much that You stand on the porch of our lives, waiting for us to return, welcoming us with open arms. (Luke 15:11-20)

So, Father we pray for the strength of father-daughter relationships. We speak and declare peace and love to every bond whether broken or unbroken. Thank you for bringing wholeness and healing to the areas of our lives that we continue to hold on to. We declare that broken relationships will end, and new beginnings will take place NOW in Jesus name!

We pray for guidance and wisdom for fathers to be great examples to their daughters on how a man should treat a lady. We pray that you would unite and strengthen this bond for your glory.

In Jesus' Name,

Amen.

## *Continued Path to Wholeness*

There was a journey involved in becoming whole. It certainly doesn't happen overnight. In fact, my path to wholeness started after I was already married. And though it was not easy, it was (as you will see) necessary and the outcome, beautiful. So, what does it mean to be "whole"? To me, wholeness is different from healing. When you think about scars; some scars will heal, but you can see the evidence of the hurt. I certainly believe that scars are sometimes there to remind you of what you went through, thus giving you a testimony. We understand that much of what we go through has nothing to do with us, but more to do with the people we are destined to help walk through similar situations.

On the other hand, wholeness suggests that those things which have been lost have become restored, as if they were never broken. In other words, we may have been broken, but we don't look like what we've been through. Becoming whole allows us to position ourselves to empower others, not tear them down. There's a saying, "hurt people, hurt other people." If this is the case, we then deal with the dilemma of a cycle of hurt. Becoming whole breaks or eradicates the cycle.

As you read on, it was on my heart to share my path to wholeness with you. Because we cannot stay in a place of rejection and brokenness, I wanted to demonstrate the path I had to take in order to receive wholeness from God. As I said, it wasn't overnight, there is no "get whole quick" 12-step-program, it was work. And as you will see, it takes courage and unwavering resolve. There is someone reading this book, who needs to make the decision today to destroy that cycle of brokenness and choose wholeness so you can position yourself for greatness.

# God's Love Through My Husband

Having a loving husband has been my heart's joy. It was so easy to fall in love with Vince. He was everything that I dreamt of. He came into my life and loved me in such a sweet way. His love was so patient and gentle and kind. We fell in love very quickly and began discussing our future together almost from the very beginning. It was like our hearts just connected from the start. God blessed me with someone whose heart is just as pure mine. When we connected, our purpose connected as well. Before Vince, I was heading down the wrong path. Although I was raised in church, I felt myself slipping further away from God. I was in college, living what I thought was my best life. Partying and hanging out in the wrong environments. I dated a variety of guys, some were abusive, and others really weren't on the same page as me. Having experienced what I did with my mom and her husband, throughout my teenage and young adult life, I had promised myself that I would never settle for anything less than what was best, when it came to choosing my husband. I feel like God sent Vince when He did to prevent me from ruining my life completely. As I stated previously, it was spoken over me, that there was a call on my life. But as I grew into my teenage and college years, I lost sight of that and I wasn't following God's plan for my life. It felt like God saw the path I was heading down and decided to send me my soul mate. The one that would help to awaken my purpose and help me walk in it.

I will never forget, we met on a Monday night. My church was having a revival that evening. I hadn't been to church in a while, so my mom asked me to come support. I asked my boyfriend, at the time, to come with me, but he refused. This almost influenced me not to attend either, but I figured since I had promised my mom I'd go, I'd attend and come up with some excuse to leave early. I arrived a little before church started, sat in my seat, and stared at my phone. Suddenly, Vince walked in with his keyboard because his church was fellowshipping with us that night. He was wearing this navy-blue suit, looking so fine. It was refreshing to see such a well put together young man. The message that night made me realize that I deserved better for myself. The next day, I asked my cousin who he was and asked him to introduce us.

When we were introduced, we started dating shortly after. At that time, Vince was serving in ministry which was a little intimidating at first. It was difficult, initially, to be with him knowing how serious his relationship with God was. At this time, I kind of felt as though he probably would have been better off choosing someone who could fully understand the calling that was on his life. Someone who had a closer relationship with God. Even though we connected so amazingly, I didn't want to let him down because I felt that I could never adequately walk alongside him in ministry. But God reminded me that there is no one else who could understand the call on his life but me. God also knew that connecting with Vince would push me to tap into my purpose. We knew that it was God who had brought us together. I helped bring out things in him that he didn't know were there, and he helped me discover things about my purpose as well which helped us both understand that God has a great plan for our lives.

So, after 1 year of dating, he asked me to marry him. I was so ecstatic about marrying Vince! Our engagement lasted 1 year, and then we got married. Our love was so breathtaking that we wanted to spend every moment together. We would pray together, share our intimate thoughts with one another, and encourage and cover one another. After seeing my mom go through the things she had experienced in her marriage, I knew I wanted something totally different, something beautiful that would last forever. We wanted our children to have two amazing parents that love each other. And that he was; Vince was (and still is) my everything outside of God. I feel like in some ways, he saved me from the brokenness I experienced growing up. This was my opportunity to build my beautiful life with my wonderful husband. Vince and I got married at a very young age. We fell in love and wanted to start our life together quickly, so baby #1 came shortly after we got married. This is what we wanted but I don't think either of us realized all that would come with starting a young family so quickly.

Things changed rapidly for us, we were newly married and now had a baby girl as well. All of that, while still trying to grow together as a couple. When we had our first baby, our time with each other took a back seat as our focus was mainly on her. She became my main priority, and ministry became more of a priority for Vince. During this time, we had many moments when we no longer put our needs first as individuals and as a couple. I felt that his ministry come before me and our family. And, for him, once I had the baby many times I put her first. Thinking back, I believe this was out of fear because I never wanted her to feel unloved by me. We were so focused on other things, not pertaining to our marriage, which gave room for the enemy to step in. Of course, with so much love and purpose in a relationship, the enemy would try and attack us. We were so young and immature in our walk with Christ that we could not even recognize the attacks coming our way. After 5 years of marriage, things started being revealed. We recognized that the enemy was attacking our thoughts, we struggled badly in our marriage for the first 5 years.

I was focused on Kayla, trying to be the best mom I could be. Because of what I went through, I wanted to give my baby everything. I was so busy putting my attention on her that I didn't notice the attacks that were coming for my husband. I was so spiritually immature. That whole time, he was struggling with the spirit of lust, which eventually led to infidelity in our marriage. Then his act of infidelity led me to be unfaithful as well. This was the worst time in our marriage and brought so much pain. I was so broken I didn't know how I was going to survive that season in our lives. But, often, it takes brokenness to birth the opportunity of being made whole by God.

I honestly believe going through that situation in our marriage was what finally caused me to desire a more intimate relationship with God. I was left devastated when I found out, we both felt lost and devastated. In that moment being a few months pregnant with our second child was the only thing that kept me from walking away. When I told him about my moment of retaliation, it left him just as broken as I was. In my humanity, I wanted him to be just as broken as I was. But the one thing in that season that made me love him more was his heart for reconciliation. Vince wanted to make it right. He was in ministry and the integrity he carried pushed him to sit his own self down to work out his issues. He didn't want to minister to people being broken himself. My admiration for my husband grew all the more because you don't see that much integrity nowadays.

Yes, this was the man God sent, and He was the One who brought us together, so I wondered how God could allow this to happen. This was a question that haunted me for years. So, of course, I had lots of questions for Vince. Sometimes, I would even ask the same questions more than once which really frustrated him at times. However, he came to a point of showing me his commitment to us becoming whole again. The enemy wanted to destroy me, my husband, and my family. I sought after God so hard, understanding that He was the only One that could make this pain go away. As hurt and as disappointed as I was with my husband, I still loved him; and he still loved me. And, most importantly, God still loved us regardless of the mistakes we made. I began to cover my husband in prayer and pray that spirit off of him. God started speaking to me to help me understand how and why this happened. This was something we had to experience as a part of our testimony. God then showed me our purpose and what we are called to accomplish together. My husband was so ashamed of his actions, he felt unworthy of my love and God's love. We both couldn't believe that our actions caused us so much pain. Above all, it was painful knowing that we had let God down. I'm so grateful that God's love never fails, He dealt with us and helped us understand that His love is unconditional. We both had moments of repenting and asking God to forgive us. God began to repair what was broken and we were able to start the path to healing, which would in no way be easy. The healing path was very rough at times. I would find myself speaking things out of my mouth that continued to hurt and diminish my husband's growth. At first, we argued a lot because, if I thought something negative, I would make it my reality even if it wasn't true. The turning point for me was when he said, "You keep coming at me like I'm still in that phase, I'd be better off doing something wrong. But I'm not because I'm focused on my growth." He said, "You don't have to believe in my deliverance, but I do." Suddenly, that moment and those words took the focus off the mistake and put it on our healing.

God helped me understand that He equipped me to handle this and that I would get through this season. He affirmed that my husband would love me more than he ever did before. God reminded me of the love we had for each other in the beginning and how we said we would never let anything come between us. This experience built some major walls that needed to be torn down and it truly humbled us both. You see, even Jesus had to learn through the things He suffered, so we chalked up a lot of this experience to - this is what we needed to learn. Up until this moment when you're reading this, we had only shared our experiences with a select few, especially with those couples whom we had the opportunity to help guide back on the right path. God allowed us to go through this painful experience alone not really having anyone to walk with us. We had to suffer privately and rebuild our marriage. In doing so, this built something wonderful and strong within us. We understood that this had nothing to do with us. But all the people we would later in life get to help and walk through tough situations. God is so amazing because, in this ordeal, God gave us a brand-new love for each other which was greater than anything we had before. My relationship with God grew and grew, He reminded me that my trust lies only with Him. My trust grew, the more I stopped trying to control the outcome of everything in our relationship.

Think of the difference between driving and riding as a passenger. I don't mind going fast as long as I'm driving, but I can get fearful if someone else is doing the same, so I constantly try to control how they drive. That's how trusting is: being content and not fearful while sitting in the passenger seat and letting God take the wheel of our lives and take us through every situation we face. In this, I also struggled to forgive because I failed to trust him. I thought forgiveness and trust were one in the same. But I had to learn the major difference between forgiveness and trust. Forgiveness is not about the person who committed the hurt, rather it's about the person being hurt. Forgiveness has a way of freeing you from the weight of the hurt. Trusting on the other hand is more like believing in someone so much that it gives you a sense of security. Just because you forgive someone doesn't mean you have to trust them. Remember forgiveness should be automatic, but trust is earned. God also reminded me that I am to pray and cover my husband and family. It took this horrible thing happening to me for me to understand my role as a wife and mother. Understanding that we must keep prayer in our home because God is the only One who can keep my marriage whole and protect my family.

Vince also had many moments with God, which allowed him to grow in a way that was simply mind blowing. He was at a place where he never wanted to allow the enemy to attack him again. This was a process in itself. During this season of restoration, we had to learn a lot on our own. We were very young in ministry and, at that time, we had no real accountability that could help guide us during this season. We struggled alone. Sometimes I wish that someone would have prepared us for all the pitfalls, tricks, and traps we would encounter. So, when we experienced this, it was a total shock. I questioned how this kind of thing could happen to someone whom I've seen God use and minister through. Unfortunately, the lack of accountability forced us to struggle alone, heal alone, and rebuild alone. But we also understand that the enemy is always waiting for an opportunity to attack. That's why this season taught us how to stay prayed up and recognize the attacks before they come. Our relationship with God is everything to us; because of this, our relationship with each other is everything. And we work hard to keep it that way. Now, we can confidently walk in our purpose and do what God has called us to do which is why God connected us from the very beginning. My husband and I both have amazing hearts that want to please God in everything we do. That rough season just helped us go hard for God in a major way. And we've been on fire ever since, understanding that the enemy isn't just going to sit back and let us be great. But we trust and understand that God has us. We are committed to one another and to doing God's will for our lives. We are so grateful for these painful moments because they produced so much greatness within us. Because of our testimony, we have helped so many people and changed many lives.

## *A Prayer for Marriage*

Dear Father,

In the name of Jesus, bless this union. Allow us to become one. Allow us to always keep God first in our lives. God, we thank You that You fill us with the ability to always communicate with one another.

Allow us to understand that in order for us to continue to grow, we always need to connect with each other, pray together, and love each other unconditionally.

Father, in the name of Jesus, we decree that we will be filled with intimacy. We declare that we remember to show affection towards each other, to be attentive to one another, and to be understanding even in our differences. We pray that a hedge of protection be placed around us, and that we are covered by the blood of Jesus.

Heavenly Father, allow us to always live our lives united as one, never competing but always complimenting. We declare that our souls intertwine and that we walk as one, joined together under the promises of God through the vows we have spoken over our marriage. In the name of Jesus, we decree to always have each other's back as we support our individual purposes that God has called us to fulfill. We decree to always be sure to encourage, uplift, and support one another. As parents, we stand united and rest assured that our commitment to each other will stand firm as we raise up children in the ways of God, the knowledge of God, the power of God, and the presence of God. Father God, we decree that we will love each other with an unconditional love that cannot be broken by circumstances but built up with an unshakeable faith in the knowledge that the Lord works all things together for our good. May the Lord keep us, protect us, provide for us, and walk with us as we experience a forever love that can never be broken because it is built on the everlasting word of God that shall live forever in us and through us, in Jesus' name we pray. Amen.

# Motherhood & Loving Others

In Proverbs 22:6 the Bible tells us to train up a child in the ways they should go and, when they are old, they will not turn from it. I have a strong desire to see my kids go further than me, so I go above and beyond to make sure they have what I never had. I have always had a desire to be a mother and truly feel this is part of my calling. I cherish the opportunity to love my children and put their needs above my own. Honestly, sometimes that feeling makes me overprotective; and the danger in being overprotective is that it could result in sheltering them from their own experiences. Being a mother is my greatest accomplishment. I chose to love my kids with everything that I have, even in my brokenness and in my pain. Being a mother is such a great gift, and I know that I'm called to be a mother. Although, growing up, I didn't have the best example on how to be a mom, I was determined to be the best mom that I could be. I often pray for patience and understanding. I pray for

God to reveal their purpose to me so that I can understand what they're called to do in this world and help them confidently walk into their purpose. As their mom, I want to ensure that all their dreams and desires come to pass.

My goal is to raise up kind-hearted children who love God and love themselves. My prayer is that my children can look at me and say, "My mommy is amazing." And for my girls to say, "I want to be just like my mom." For my son to say, "I want to be like my daddy." We want any and all generational curses to stop and end with us. Our children are our first priority, though I know we can't shield them from everything. I know they will have to go through some things and make their own share of mistakes to learn from. But as their parents we work hard to make sure we're not inflicting pain on them. I know as parents were not always going to get it right, but we strive to put them first and love them with our whole hearts.

Being a mom comes very natural to me, but sometimes the way I yell at them reminds me of how my mother talked to me. She never took the time to listen to me. Likewise, I remember fussing at my oldest daughter about something and she came to me hours later to talk about what happened. At first, I wanted to push it off, but then I caught myself and took the time to listen to what she had to say. I always promised myself that I would be a mom whom my children could feel comfortable talking to about anything. My babies have been the greatest gift that God could have ever given me. Psalm 127:3 where it states that children are a heritage from the Lord, and offspring a reward from Him; this is very real for me.

I've always showed love to others very easily as the Bible says to in 1 John 4:7 where the Apostle John tell us to love one another for love comes from God. God has given me such an amazing heart. I consistently try to see the good in people, although many times doing so came back to bite me. There were times I got hurt because I trusted people so easily but that has always been my heart to show love. Often, when people turn on me and hurt me, I would ask God why this would keep happening. And God would remind me that I'm to love people unto God because that's what He requires of me. So, when people walk away or hurt me, I'm not devastated. That really helped me understand how to continue loving even when it was not easy. God allowed me to show my love for someone else in the most amazing way, which has truly blessed my life so much.

God allowed me to open my home to my cousin's daughter who was in foster care. Having a heart for people; I saw this as an opportunity to give her something that I didn't have at her age. I chose to take in this 10-year-old, because I was close to her age when my mom left me, and I felt abandoned and alone. I wanted to help make a difference in her life, I wanted her to feel loved. I wanted her to feel like she belonged to something special. And I wanted her experience with me to be something that she should remember forever. Hoping this would be a highlight in her time in foster care. I really wanted to make an impact by building her up when her circumstances could potentially tear her down. This came with its own set of challenges because there were ramifications from her time in foster care. So, it was difficult raising her within the standards of our household. To a degree it became difficult raising our own kids because of the guidelines the state places on families. Ways of disciplining our own children had to adjust so we didn't traumatize our foster child. Overall, we wanted to make sure we were giving her the love, safe environment, and sense of belonging I felt I needed at that age.

Helping her discover her purpose and understand that God loves her no matter what her circumstance is at this moment gave us a new sense of purpose as well. I know the emptiness that I felt when I couldn't be with my mom. I know what it's like to feel as if no one understands me. Bringing her into my home not only gave her a safe environment where she could grow and experience love and happiness; but also, loving her helped me personally heal in many ways. Loving her brought me so much joy knowing that I was making a difference in this little girl's life. Showing love to others has always been my way of healing, allowing God's unconditional love for me to help me heal. Giving Aaliyah, who was in foster care, the love and care that I desired at her age, helped my heart to heal. I truly thank God for the heart that He has given me for His people. And for being obedient to God and loving others even when it's not easy to do so.

The difficulty sometimes in loving others is the risk you take of that love not being reciprocated. For me, I know that God has given me the ability to love in any situation. Sometimes, I put others' feelings before my own and I'm the one left hurt by people whose love for me is conditional. One thing that I learned is that you don't have to necessarily like a person, but God asks that we love everyone. Because of this, I'm able to walk in my wholeness, not focusing on the opinions of others or their perception of me. I have decided not to stay in a place of brokenness. I now can enjoy the beautiful life and family that God has blessed me with. I could not ask for better children or a better husband they love me so much. I'm totally fulfilled in my life; God not only gave me my dream family, but I now also have the greatest relationship with my father and mother. I have such an amazing squad of people in my life. Because of my kind heart, He has blessed me with 4 amazing sisters in Christ. I have always wanted a big sister and God gave me four. These women have been everything to me, God definitely sent them into my life to help me walk in my purpose. They have loved and prayed me through some of the toughest experiences in my life. So grateful for my "Yes" to God and walking in obedience and doing what God requires of me. Though it was not at all easy, because of this, He has blessed me with the greatest relationships with the people that I love. I'm now fully walking in my wholeness. I know there may be many more moments that will try to come and break me, but

I'm committed to the peace that only wholeness can bring.

## *A Prayer for Families*

Heavenly Father,
In the name of Jesus, I lift up families before You. To every family that's represented in the pages of this book, and to the family of every reader, I speak life and peace. Dear God, breathe upon each family refreshing, renewing, and reconciliation. Encourage families to walk in unconditional love toward one another. Help us to be patient with our families, kind and worthy of trust. I plead the blood of Jesus right now over every family, and I cancel every demonic assignment. I declare that no weapon formed against them shall prosper.

Father God, help families to walk in forgiveness, never holding grudges nor walking in offense. Remind every family that there is power in the words that we speak. Holy Spirit please guide our tongue, so that we build one another up and not tear each other down. I speak a fresh revival into families, dear Lord, full of beautiful memories, fun, and enjoyment. Help families recognize the importance of making time for one another, for we know that tomorrow is not promised. Holy Spirit help us to hide Your Word in our hearts, as we remember to pray sincerely and earnestly for our family. For God, we stand on Your promise, that if we would humble ourselves, pray, and seek Your face, that You would hear from heaven and heal our land.

In Jesus' name, amen.

Made in the USA
Monee, IL
24 May 2021